LONDONDERRY & LOUGH SWILLY RAILWAY

An Irish Railway Pictorial

Steve Flanders
in association with
Joe Begley and Hugh Dougherty

Midland Publishing
Limited

This book is dedicated to all those who are striving to recreate something of the spirit and atmosphere of the narrow gauge railways that once ran through County Donegal, and to all those who have worked so tenaciously to preserve that which remains of this wonderful part of Ireland's railway heritage.

To everyone who is working to restore the best of the past for the benefit of the future we can do no better than quote a CDR railcar driver who recently told us that being employed by the railways in Donegal meant that you had to 'work hard and spend no money foolishly!' Aye, well said!

The Londonderry & Lough Swilly Railway
© 1997 Steve Flanders, Joe Begley and Hugh Dougherty

ISBN 1 85780 073 7

Published by
Midland Publishing Limited
24 The Hollow, Earl Shilton
Leicester, LE9 7NA, England
Tel: 01455 847815 Fax: 01455 841805
E-mail: midlandbooks@compuserve.com

Design concept and layout
© Midland Publishing Limited
and Stephen Thompson Associates.

Printed and bound in England by
Woolnough Bookbinding Limited
Irthlingborough, Northamptonshire

Photographs on the front cover:

This busy scene in front of Pennyburn shed dates from May 1938. Among the locomotives are Nos 5, 8, 14 and 16. Behind No 16 on the centre road is 4-8-0 No 12, without its tender. H C Casserley

This was how the former L&LSR station at Letterkenny looked in 1958. Swilly road freight vehicles are on the trackbed and just visible on the extreme left of the picture, is a Lough Swilly bus. Still officially a railway company, though one without track or trains, the L&LSR logo on the open door of the Bedford lorry is similar to the device applied to the locomotives in the final years of railway operations. Keith Bannister

Title page photograph:
Company staff pose outside the station on Strand Road, Londonderry, 1923.

INTRODUCTION

THE catchment area of the railway companies that were to eventually become the Londonderry & Lough Swilly Railway was all that area of County Donegal extending from Derry westwards to Letterkenny and beyond, and northwards to either side of Lough Swilly itself. This vast region comprises large stretches of good farmland bounded by steep hills and mountains on peninsulas deeply cut by sea loughs. West of Letterkenny the north-east to south-west grain of the granite mountains are suitable only for sheep and, on their seawards fringe, for fishing and subsistence cultivation. In all, a most unlikely setting for a railway, yet it was through this very countryside that Ireland's second largest narrow gauge railway network was built, and one on which some of the most impressive steam engines to operate on the Irish narrow gauge ran. From the outset, the L&LSR was cash-strapped. Extensions relied on Government grants; economies enforced by the Board of Works in constructing and equipping the extensions affected operation and ultimately led to the demise of railway services.

From the early 1920s, the L&LSR management realised that the company's financial and operating future lay in road transport to which they transferred at the earliest opportunity, unlike the County Donegal Railway in the south of the county which battled for so long to maintain rail services. But how did a railway come to be built in such an unlikely location in the first place? To answer this question, we must return to the mid-nineteenth century when a railway for the area was first proposed.

Derry, at this time, had developed as an important trade centre and the major port for the north-west corner of Ireland. Improvements in communication between Derry and the district surrounding Lough Swilly had long been considered and from the mid-eighteenth century, a number of proposals for the construction of a canal connecting Lough Foyle with Lough Swilly were mooted. This was a period when coastal shipping was often quicker than overland transport and the sea loughs of Ireland were important arteries for trade of all types. Indeed, many of the small towns along the shores of Lough Swilly had much better contact with Glasgow, by boat, than with Dublin, by cart.

The canal project was only part of the overall improvements considered. A large area of low-lying land opposite Inch Island was regularly inundated by the tides and plans were laid to build lengthy embankments to reclaim many hundreds of acres for farming. Accordingly, between 1838 and 1850 four massive embankments were constructed. These were the Trady embankment linking Burnfoot to Trady Island; the Blanket Nook embankment just north of Newtoncunningham; and the two stretching across the lough to Inch Island – from Quigley's Point and from just east of Farland Point respec-

tively. Altogether they reclaimed from the sea almost 3,000 acres of land.

The canal was to have been an integral part of this scheme but a combination of cost, engineering difficulties associated with the varying tidal ranges of the two loughs, and the rapid growth of railways elsewhere led to its abandonment. Instead, a number of railway routes were proposed. The one to succeed was that promoted by the Lough Foyle & Lough Swilly Railway Company whose Act of Incorporation was granted in June 1853, by which time the company had renamed itself the Londonderry & Lough Swilly Railway Company.

The L&LSR proposed to run a line from the quayside at Derry along the *Skeoge River* valley as far as Burnfoot and then along the top of the Trady embankment to Farland Point where there would be steamer connections throughout the lough and beyond. Construction eventually commenced in 1860, the line being built to the Irish standard gauge of 5ft 3in. While under construction, it was decided to make a junction just west of Burnfoot and to then turn northwards along the coast to Buncrana.

The line to Farland Point opened on the very last day of 1863 and that to Buncrana sometime towards the end of the following year. Unfortunately, the service to Farland Point was very little used, steamer timings not being under the railway company's control. By contrast the line to Buncrana flourished. As a consequence, in 1866, after only three years' service, the Farland Point branch was abandoned and the L&LSR concentrated all its services on the line to Buncrana.

Since the mid-1850's, several projects had been mooted to connect the important town of Letterkenny to the railway network. Two routes were considered. One was for a branch leaving the Londonderry & Enniskillen Railway's line running alongside the *River Foyle* at Cuttyman hill following a westward route. The other was for a line from the L&LSR's abandoned track at Farland Point south-westwards via Manorcunningham and Pluck.

After some 20 years of discussion and delay, the latter route was decided upon. The unusual difficulties in raising the capital were overcome when Baronial guarantees were secured, the rate payers in the districts served by the line undertaking to guarantee the interest on the money used to built it. The Letterkenny Railway Company was incorporated in 1860. In an effort to further reduce costs it was decided to build the line to the 3ft gauge. Accordingly, the Letterkenny Railway Company's narrow gauge line from Tooban Junction to Letterkenny was opened in 1883. The L&LSR remained standard gauge for a further two years so that a change of trains and gauges was always necessary at the junction. In 1885 the logical decision was taken and the L&LSR re-gauged to 3ft. Buncrana services were suspended for the first week of April 1885 while the work took place. The result was a unified narrow gauge network some 31 miles long and consisting of two lines linking important towns to the city of Derry.

The line to Letterkenny was nominally independent but was worked by the L&LSR. By 1887, after only four years of operation, failure to repay the interest on government loans resulted in the Letterkenny company being wound up and the line being taken over by the Board of Works. The L&LSR agreed to continue to work the line and so began the company's chequered association with the Board.

The last decade or so of the nineteenth century saw many plans for further expansion but it wasn't until the Government offered funding for the building of railways in the so-called 'congested' areas that any new lines were built. The Congested Districts Act of 1891 sought to improve the economic condition of the poorest areas, those where the land was deemed too poor to support the people who lived there, hence the term 'congested'. Fishing was encouraged as were improvements in communication between the fishing ports and the main towns and cities. For the Swilly it meant the construction of two lines, an extension north to Carndonagh from Buncrana first proposed in 1885, and the long winding line to far-off Burtonport on the Atlantic coast where it was hoped that harbour improvements would stimulate the fishing industry.

Though both extensions were jointly planned by the Board of Works and the L&LSR, the former, as the paymaster insisted on a number of economies, the search for which resulted in frustrating delays for the company. Nevertheless, the Carndonagh line proceeded relatively smoothly, opening in July 1901. Built entirely with grant aid, with the L&LSR supplying rolling stock, the line took the only significant pass through the mountains, north-eastwards from Buncrana Station to Drumfries, then veered north-west to Clonmany and Ballyliffin. From here it followed the coast before turning east and then south-east to terminate at Carndonagh.

The Burtonport line was built by a separate concern, the Letterkenny & Burtonport Extension Railway. The use above of the word 'concern' is deliberate. The L&BER was not an independent company, its actual status, other than as a vehicle to build the line, is imprecise. Its name appeared on the stock bought by the Board of Works for use on the extension. Perhaps this was to provide visual evidence to civil servants that government property was being misused, if these vehicles were seen elsewhere on the Swilly system, as they often were. This was one item on a long agenda of claims and counter-claims which soured relations between the L&LSR and the Board of Works in the years after the Burtonport line was built.

The economies pursued in the construction of the Burtonport line had more serious consequences. Its objective was to link the fishing port with the rest of Ireland's railway network by the shortest route possible. Consequently, the line first ran west then north of Letterkenny as far as Creeslough where it again swung westwards towards Errigal, threading a path through the mountains and moorlands to Gweedore and Burtonport. The route chosen to get to Burton-

port meant that, despite traversing almost 50 miles of the county the railway managed to avoid most of the coastal settlements, at best they were served by stations two or three miles away. From the outset, therefore the Burtonport line was disadvantaged in attracting whatever modest passenger traffic there might be in the thinly populated area which it served. Most of the population of north-west Donegal lived on the coast which the line avoided and not the interior which it passed through. It was reliant on whatever goods traffic it could win: that there was little enough of this, was a significant factor in the line's subsequent demise. The company were also unhappy about many aspects of the line's construction and the rolling stock provided by the Board, believing them to be inadequate. Despite these difficulties, the line passed its Board of Trade inspection and opened in March 1903. However, relations with the Board soon reached an all time low. The service on the Burtonport Extension was poor and the L&LSR bitterly complained that this was due to enforced economies in the building and equipping of the line. Claim followed counter claim until in 1909, Sir Charles Scotter agreed to mediate between the L&LSR, the Board and the Treasury, the outcome being the 'Scotter Award' whereby some improvements in rolling stock and facilities on the line were obtained.

The early decades of the century saw the railway activities of the L&LSR at their peak with some 99 miles of narrow gauge line, a developing fleet of locomotives and new coaching and goods stock. Steamers operated up and down the lough and connected with trains at Fahan pier, the services to Rathmullen, Ramelton and Portsalon being the most popular. The steamer company was owned by McRea and McFarland and was never controlled by the railway company. This apparent golden age for the Swilly must however be put into perspective. Successive examinations and enquiries raised doubts about safety and working practices while income never generated sufficient profit to provide any reasonable dividends for the shareholders.

Ireland's struggle for independence after the First World War also left its mark. Trains were often hired to transport British troops. Staff frequently refused to operate them either through conviction or intimidation. The railway itself was attacked and damaged to prevent troop trains from running and on at least one occasion a mail train with plain-clothed British agents on board was attacked and a running gun fight ensued. Following partition, the war of independence continued as a civil war between those who supported the truncated 26 county Free State and those who continued the fight for independence for the whole 32 counties of Ireland. Throughout the L&LSR's area, this war was hard fought and many incidents involved the railway until hostilities largely ended in 1925. A further complication caused by partition was the introduction of customs checks. Lough Swilly trains now had to cross an international frontier at which two sets of customs officials had the opportunity to practice their machismo.

The 1920s and '30s proved to be the crunch period for the Swilly. Further south the County Donegal Railway was already successfully utilising first petrol and then diesel powered railcars but this option was not taken up by the L&LSR directors. Instead, they viewed the general decline in railway revenue as an indicator that the company's future lay with road transport and accordingly began to acquire road vehicles.

In 1935 the retrenchment of railway services began with the closure of the Cardonagh line north of Buncrana after only 34 years of service. At the same time the road transport fleet rapidly expanded and, it must be admitted, the financial health of the company improved. Dividends of 5% now became possible and these were to grow to 7% as further railway routes were replaced by bus services. The Burtonport line was closed in 1940 and was already being ripped up when there was a stay of execution caused by wartime fuel shortages. The line at least as far as Gweedore, stayed open for goods traffic only for another seven years.

By 1947 only the Letterkenny line had a passenger service though goods trains continued to run to Buncrana. The buses had virtually won! And small wonder, as at least they actually went into the little towns and villages rather than giving them a passing nod from a hillside several miles away. On 1st July 1953, the last train crossed the Strand Road and pulled into Graving Dock Station in Londonderry. Few were present to witness the end of the railway. The company went over entirely to road transport and has since then continued as a major passenger and freight haulier in north Donegal with its buses still a familiar sight on the county's roads.

Locomotives and Rolling Stock

Over the years the Swilly owned and operated some of the most powerful locomotives to be found on the Irish 3ft narrow gauge but all were scrapped when the line finally closed in 1953.

All six of the original locomotives used on the standard gauge system were 0-6-0 tank engines. After re-gauging, these were no longer of any use and they were either scrapped or sold. Nos 4 *St Patrick* and 5 *St Columb* were sold to the Cork, Bandon & South Coast Railway where they were converted to 4-4-0T engines. Nothing is known of the livery of these engines.

For the opening of the Letterkenny Railway in 1883, the Swilly ordered three 0-6-2 tank engines from Black, Hawthorn & Company. The first engine, No 1 *J.T. Mackey,* arrived in 1882. It later was hired for use in the construction of the Clogher Valley Railway and the CDR's Glenties branch. It was scrapped in 1911. Two similar engines, No 2 *Londonderry* and No 3 *Donegal* followed in 1883, remaining in service until 1912 and 1913 respectively. No 4 *Inishowen,* an 0-6-0 side-tank locomotive arrived in 1885, also from Black, Hawthorn & Company. For a while, the leading section of its coupling rods were removed, making it a 2-4-0T. It was extensively rebuilt and renumbered No 17, around 1914 and though it lost its name at this time, it survived in this form until 1940.

In 1885 two 2-4-0T locomotives arrived from the Glenariff Iron Ore & Harbour Company in Antrim. They had the distinction of being the first 3ft gauge engines in Ireland, built by Robert Stephenson & Company in 1873. Numbered 5 and 6, they served for only 14 years, being placed in reserve at Pennyburn in 1899 as Nos 5a and 6a before being scrapped some short time afterwards.

The need for greater power on the Carndonagh Extension led to the introduction of what was to become the most popular wheel arrangement used by the Swilly, the 4-6-2 tank. Eight examples of this type were acquired from three different builders. The first pair were supplied by Hudswell Clarke & Company of Leeds in 1899, costing £1,850 each (works numbers 518 & 519). They took the now vacant numbers 5 and 6, though they were later renumbered 15 and 16 in 1913. Acquired for the opening of the Carndonagh branch, they were used at first on the Letterkenny line, a fact which led to legal proceedings by the Board of Works which had paid for them. Once the new line opened on 1st July 1901, they took on the work for which they had been provided. Both survived to the end of rail services, though No 16 had been out of use for a number of years. No 15 had the sad task of working the last passenger train into Derry on 8th August 1953.

Two more 4-6-2 tanks from Hudswell Clarke & Company followed in March and April, 1901 (works numbers 562 and 577), costing £2,100 each and numbered 7 and 8. These were virtually identical to the original pair, the only significant modification being the introduction of Allan Straight motion (the only Irish application). No 8 lasted up till 1953, still in running order, and was finally cut up in the spring of 1954. No 7 hauled the Royal Train in July 1903, for which it was named *Edward VII*. It had frequent heavy repairs in the 1920s and was scrapped in 1936.

For the Burtonport Extension, a batch of four 4-6-0 tanks were purchased from Andrew Barclay Sons & Company in 1902 by the Board of Works. These are believed to be inspired by and were virtually identical to the class 2 4-6-0Ts of the County Donegal Railway.

The Swilly argued that the fuel capacity of these engines, together with the inadequate watering facilities on the extension, made them unsuitable for use on the Burtonport line. Despite this they were excellent and reliable engines. Numbered 1 to 4 they survived to the end with the exception of No 1 which was scrapped in 1940.

Two further 4-6-2 tank locomotives arrived in 1904 this time from Kerr Stuart & Company (works numbers 845 and 846). They were given the numbers 9 and 10 and named *Aberfoyle* and *Richmond,* though the names were removed about ten years later. They worked mainly on the Derry to Letterkenny line, No 9 surviving only until 1927 though No 10 lasted to the end.

The next engines to arrive were the most notable members of the fleet, the two 4-8-0 tender engines, Nos 11 and 12. They had the dis-

tinction of being the only tender engines ever to run on an Irish narrow gauge line. They were also the first engines in Ireland to have eight coupled wheels and the only tender engines of this wheel arrangement to run anywhere in the British Isles. They were built in 1905 by Hudswell Clarke & Company of Leeds at a cost of £2,750 each. No 11 was already worn out by 1928 and was scrapped in 1933. No 12 lasted to the end, though there was little work for her after the closure of the Burtonport line.

The next pair of engines, again of the 4-6-2 tank wheel arrangement, were purchased in 1910 from Hawthorn Leslie & Company Limited, at a cost of £2,050 each (works numbers 2801 and 2802). Numbered 13 and 14, they were given additional water capacity to enable them to work through to Burtonport. This, however, made them top heavy, with a high centre of gravity, causing them to roll a lot at speed and giving an uncomfortable ride to the crews. They were also poor steamers and heavy on coal.

No 14 was the engine involved in the Owencarrow viaduct disaster of January 1925. She was scrap-ped in 1943. No 13 was maliciously derailed and damaged in 1921. She had a history of heavy repairs and was finally scrapped in 1940.

The last two engines to be acquired were two 4-8-4T locomotives, like the 4-8-0, these were the only steam engines with this wheel arrangement to work in these islands. Supplied by Hudswell Clarke in 1912 at a cost of £2,765 each, they were, essentially, a tank version of two 4-8-0 tender engines and assumed the numbers 5 and 6 previously carried by the 1873 built 2-4-0Ts. They were the most powerful engines ever to run on the Irish 3ft gauge and the pride of the Swilly. Officially acquired for the Burtonport Extension, they were often to be found on heavy passenger trains on the Derry to Buncrana route. No 6 was subject to a number of heavy repairs, including a major overhaul at the CDR's workshop in Stranorlar. Both officially survived until the end, though in later years they seldom left Pennyburn. No 5 was employed on lifting trains following closure. Both were advertised for sale in running condition, but found no buyers and were subsequently cut up.

The Swilly did request the loan of one of the CDR's class 5a 2-6-4T tank engines for trials in 1922. It appears this was with a view to acquiring new engines. However, the request was refused and, in fact, no further motive power was ordered.

Early livery on narrow gauge engines was a bright green with red buffer beams on which the number was painted in yellow. However, between the wars, they were repainted black as overhaul became due, with a variety of lining schemes, some remaining unlined. By 1940 they were beginning to revert to green, although the actual shade, and lining pattern, varied from locomotive to locomotive. In later years, the distinctive Swilly logo, a diamond shaped outline containing the ornate lettering 'LSR' was added to some. The Burtonport stock bore simple L&BER lettering.

Carriages, vans and wagons

While some of the locomotives on the Swilly may have been the most impressive and powerful ever to grace the 3ft gauge, the same cannot be said of the passenger coaching stock. The carriages were rather shabby, invariably in need of repair, a good coat of paint and general tidy up. Some of the earliest 6-wheel coaches remained in service right through to closure by which time they were really showing their age. Seating was uncomfortable, being mostly of the wooden slatted type.

The Swilly neglected to provide other simple creature comforts, such as heating – steam heating was never installed. A small quantity of foot warmers were supplied to passengers from time to time and even these came second-hand from the Midland Great Western Railway. A further 29 were later bought from the County Donegal Railway. Carriages were initially lit by oil lamps and, later, by acetylene gas burners mounted through holes in the roof with gas lighting generators housed in a metal box on one end of the carriage. As these eventually wore out, they were replaced by electric lights powered from batteries, which came from the Swilly's growing fleet of road buses.

Not a lot can be said about the rolling stock used in the early standard gauge days as no photographs or drawings are extant. This lack of documentation is probably due to the fact that the rolling stock was hired by the Swilly from a local businessman John Cooke and, later, from the contractor McCormick who was responsible for ballasting the track. These individuals came to the aid of the Swilly when the company was not then in a position to pay for the rolling stock it had ordered.

In contrast, the L&LSR had a large selection of narrow gauge rolling. At the peak, around 1930, the company possessed a total of 317 assorted vans, wagons and carriages. Records of the narrow gauge stock are again poor and complicated by the fact that stock used on the Burtonport Extension was numbered separately. Indeed, at one time no less than six separate series of numbering existed. To complicate matters further damaged or worn out vehicles were recycled reappearing in a different guise, coaches rebuilt as goods vans for example. This extended their useful working life and was a practice common, though better documented, on the neighbouring CDR system.

All Swilly coaches were wooden framed with timber planked sides and built on a metal chassis. The first carriages from Oldbury Carriage & Wagon Company were six wheelers, numbered 1 to 22 and supplied between 1884 and 1899. Nos 1, 4, 6 to 19 and 22 were 3rds, Nos 2, 3, 5 and 21 were 1st/2nd composites and No 20 was a tri-composite. None of these vehicles had any luggage or brake compartments. They were all divided into five separate passenger compartments. Seven of these carriages were damaged in the Springtown accident of 1891. No 12 was damaged in the Owencarrow accident of 1925. Dates of withdrawal are uncertain, though a 1925 census omits Nos 9 and 14 to 16.

Thirteen bogie coaches, Nos 23 to 35 were purchased from the Lancaster Railway Carriage & Wagon Company in 1901, for the opening of the Carndonagh Line. Of these, Nos 23, 26 to 29 and 35 were 6-compartment 3rds, Nos 25 and 32 to 34 were Brake/3rds and Nos 24, 30 and 31 were tri-composites. Again little is known of withdrawal dates. Most of the series underwent major rebuilds in the 1920s. No 23 was converted to a hut in Pennyburn in the late 1930s.

For the opening of the Burtonport Extension, 12 bogie carriages were purchased from Pickerings of Wishaw in 1903. A thirteenth followed in 1910. They were numbered 1 to 13 in a separate L&BER series, with a 'B' prefix. Of these, Nos 1 to 5 and No 13 were 6-compartment 3rds, Nos 6 to 9 were Brake/3rds and Nos 10 to 12 were 6-compartment tri-composites. Carriages were painted in a variety of sombre colours over the years. At first they were adorned with dark brown above and light brown below. From 1902 the livery was changed to cream upper panels with dark red below. At some later point they were painted entirely black but finally they received a coat of light grey and which lasted until the close of the railway in 1953.

The Swilly owned a total of 110 flat wagons or timber flats as they were also known, built up with three or four plank sides. Twenty-six of these had centre doors. There were also 56 goods vans, some with parts of their roofs cut away and covered by canvas to facilitate loading by hand crane. The company's more unusual possessions included a single horse box, a mess and tool van, a stores van, a travelling crane, a stone engine and stone breaker. There were, in addition, six oil tank wagons owned by BP which were numbered in their own separate series. A total of 35 flat wagons and 51 covered vans were on the stock list of the Burtonport line, the greater number of covered vehicles highlighting the importance of the fish trade on this line.

The Course of the Line

The Derry terminus was at the Graving Dock, an uninspiring, cramped and run-down looking station. After a short run along the quay, the line crossed Strand Road by an oblique level crossing and entered Pennyburn, the site of the administrative offices and workshops. The Act of Incorporation forbade the Swilly from running engines over this crossing. The company ignored this and strictly speaking operated locomotives over the crossing illegally until 1918, when an Act permitting the construction of a new terminus at Pennyburn which was never built, also granted statutory powers for the operation of steam locomotives over the crossing.

Leaving Pennyburn, open country was soon reached and the line followed essentially a level course all the way to Buncrana, crossing the Donegal border some three miles out. Bridge End Station lay just over the border and housed the Free State customs following partition. From here the railway crossed boggy land, reclaimed from the sea by the embankments, to Tooban Junction where the line to Letterkenny turned westwards and that to Buncrana curved to the north. Continuing northwards, the line hugged the coast, passing Fahan, where the original Farland pier was re-erected in 1868, to reach Buncrana, the terminus for all but the 34 years the Carndonagh Extension was in existence.

The Carndonagh line, on leaving Buncrana, crossed the main road and the *Mill River*, curving round to the north to swing round the town towards Ballymagan. After crossing open moorland and passing Kinnego Gates it headed for the only significant pass through the mountains, north-eastwards to Drumfries, climbing continuously for seven miles at grades of up to 1 in 50. The summit, at 332ft above sea-level, was followed by a descent of four miles as the line turned north-west to Clonmany, where trains could be crossed. Another short ascent and an eastwards turn to Ballyliffen was followed by a descent to sea-level at Rashenny, the most northerly railway station in Ireland. From here the line continued eastwards to reach Carndonagh.

The Letterkenny Railway, on leaving Tooban Junction, crossed the reclaimed salt flatlands first on the Trady and then the Farland embankments, passing Carrowen Station. These were followed by a short undulating stretch to the crossing station of Newtoncunningham. After Newton came a steady three mile climb with grades of up to 1 in 60, to a summit just before Sallybrook. From here the line descended steeply into Manorcunningham. The descent continued thereafter, though in a gentler, undulating fashion, reaching level ground about a mile from Letterkenny. Here the Swilly was bridged by the CDR's Strabane & Letterkenny line coming up from the south. The two lines continued side by side to their adjoining stations in Letterkenny.

The Letterkenny & Burtonport Extension first headed in a south-westerly direction along the valley of the *Swilly River* skirting the south of the town and passing Old Town Station before sweeping west to New Mills Station. Here the line swung north-west and began a steady three mile climb at grades of up to 1 in 50. It levelled out briefly between crossing gates 2 and 3 before dipping to Church Hill Station. Further steep climbing followed through Kilmacrenan, to a summit just before Barnes Gap. This was immediately followed by a sharp descent at 1 in 50 and a tight northwards curve to the Owencarrow Viaduct. Creeslough and Dunfanaghy Road were followed by a five mile steady climb to the summit of the extension near Errigal. Thereafter, the line descended to Falcarragh before climbing to another peak at Cashelnagore Station, remotely perched on the mountainside high above Gweedore. A long undulating descent followed through Gweedore, Crolly and Dungloe Road stations as the railway swung westwards through the Rosses before terminating at the fish quay at Burtonport some 74½ miles from Londonderry.

Road Services

From the 1920s onwards, improvements in road transport coupled with the shortcomings in the construction and equipment of the lines it operated, brought the Swilly to recognise that the company's future lay in road rather than rail transport. It began acquiring road vehicles in 1931 following legislation in both jurisdictions whereby the company could buy up competing road services. The first serious moves from rail to road began in the early 1930s. An attempt to extend bus services to Dungloe and Burtonport in 1931 proved premature when roads and buses inflicted heavy damage on each other, the company receiving a large compensation claim from Donegal County Council as a result. However the country-wide rail strike of January 1933 was followed by the closing in 1934 of the Carndonagh Extension and its replacement by road services. The Irish Free State Transport Act of 1933 facilitated the takeover of a large number of goods carriers. By the end of 1935 the company owned 37 buses and 56 lorries. A period of scrapping and withdrawal of the nondescript fleet acquired from the independents it had taken over followed and during the period of the Second World War lorries were acquired as opportunity permitted so that 60 were in use by 1946 while the number of buses had fallen to 32. By 1950 the road fleet had grown to 59 lorries, four mail vans and 52 buses.

As with the railway, every possible economy was employed with road operations. Area controllers looked after both passenger and goods traffic, old station buildings were employed as local offices. Some crews took their vehicles back to their home villages rather than to the distant garage each evening. Servicing and refuelling was done at places like Letterkenny and Moville during lay-over periods. At Derry, the former railway engineering shops were adapted to supplement bus running sheds erected in 1942, when the original L&LS garage was requisitioned by the US Navy, never to be returned. As far as possible vehicles based west and north of Letterkenny, were overhauled in workshops at the station there.

Cross border operations presented some difficulties with the need for customs clearance. Schedules allowed time for this, but delays were inevitable. Special passes were required for each of the two customs posts. As a proportion of the cross-border movements took place after normal customs hours, large annual sums in supplementary fees were charged. Also, although the Swilly taxed each vehicle in the country in which it was normally stationed, they all operated at some time in the other state, and therefore had to be inspected annually by the public service vehicle inspectors from both jurisdictions. Both drivers and the conductors had to hold PSV licences for both countries and vehicle insurance had to be valid on both sides of the border. A further financial penalty was the import duty levied on road vehicles brought for the first time into the Republic – as much as 150 per cent on second-hand bodies, though less when chassis or body was imported in 'knocked-down' condition to be assembled by local labour.

In its operating area, the Swilly handled nearly all the Republic's Post Office work, drivers or conductors delivering and collecting from post offices on or close to a bus route. Mail formed a substantial part of the revenue with, from time to time, buses carrying mails alone, thus avoiding what would otherwise have been an empty trip.

Live link with the past

A real live link with the great days of the narrow gauge Londonderry & Lough Swilly Railway and very much part and parcel of everyday life of north-west Donegal, that's the Swilly of today, its vehicles still proudly lettered 'L&LS Rly', just to remind all concerned that tradition counts.

Since the railway closed in 1953, the Lough Swilly on the road has survived change and challenge in plenty. The buses were at their most railway-like during the 1960s when conductors, known as 'guards' of course, were the norm, and likely to be ex-railway staff too. Insert Setright ticket machines were in use printing card tickets which spoke of their railway ancestry.

Parcels and mail traffic was there in plenty and long queues of Swilly buses waited at the quayside at Derry for the arrival of the boat from Glasgow, to transport hundreds of returning Rosses exiles home on the last lap of their journey. The roof racks of the buses would be piled high with the belongings of these passengers. It was the same story when youngsters from Derry headed west in the Swilly buses for the summer stay in the Gaeltacht.

The last decade has seen the company change hands and it has had to fight to survive. The Swilly buses have survived the worst effects of the troubles in Northern Ireland and competition from new operators on its patch. One positive event in recent years, thanks to the advent of European Union, has been the ending of the tyranny of the customs men at the border. The Swilly is still here following on in the best traditions of the railway that gave the buses and lorries their *raison d'être* in the first place. So,

come the millennium, we hope it will still be possible to buy a return to Buncrana on the vehicles of Ireland's oldest railway company. The Swilly may have changed but it's lineage can still be traced back to that Act of Parliament of 1853 and few transport operators anywhere in these islands can boast as fine a pedigree as that!

The authors and the County Donegal Railway Restoration Society gratefully acknowledge the generosity of the many photographers whose pictures appear in these pages. By allowing the CDRRS to use their photographs free of charge they have made a direct financial contribution to our project to revive a stretch of the CDR and the maintenance of our heritage centre in the old narrow gauge station at Donegal Town. Thanks are also due to the following individuals who have both read parts of the proofs and supplied additional information which has enhanced the book; Allan T Condie, Michael Corcoran, Tom Ferris, Geoff Lumb and Des McGlynn.

GRAVING DOCK STATION

Below: **The overall roof did not extend very far up the platform as can be seen in this 1953 view which records 4-6-2T No 15 at the head of a special train which had been** organised for members of the Light Railway and Tramway League who were visiting the system. J H Price

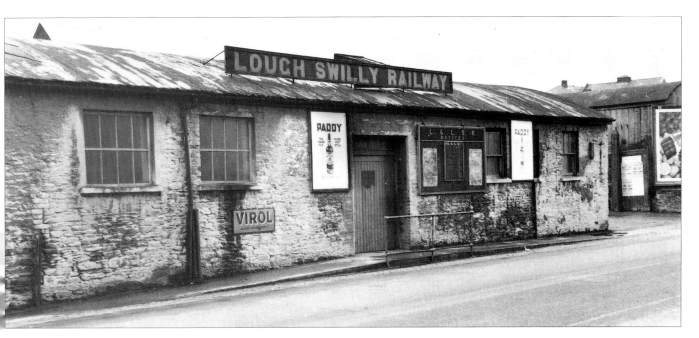

Above: **Graving Dock Station was the terminus of the Lough Swilly Railway for most of its life, being opened in 1863 and surviving until the closure of the line some 90 years later in 1953. The original building was a simple wooden shed and its replacement in 1883 was decidedly unprepossessing, having been originally built as a goods depot. For a time in the 1860s and '70s, trains ran on through to Middle Quay on the Harbour** Commissioners' lines, about a mile to the south and therefore much closer to the city centre and the Foyle Road terminus of what was to become the GNR(I) line to Strabane and Enniskillen. However there were continual arguments between the railway company and the Harbour Commissioners which in the end forced the L&LSR to make Graving Dock its passenger and goods terminus in Derry. Neil Sprinks

Below: **Elegance was not a word that could easily be associated with Graving Dock Station, its two platforms cocooned between rough walls. Passengers join a train bound for Buncrana which will be hauled by No 10 on 19th April 1948.** H C Casserley

Top left: **The goods store was relocated to the station throat when Graving Dock became a passenger station in 1883. It can be seen here behind locomotive No 2 arriving with a short freight from Letterkenny on 16th March 1953.** Willie McGowan collection

Top right: **Given the sparse population of much of the area it served, goods traffic was always important to the fortunes of the L&LSR. In this August 1952 view a locomotive is shunting outside the goods store at Graving Dock. To the right of the narrow gauge wagons in the centre of the picture can be glimpsed some Great Northern vans on the adjoining Harbour Commissioners quayside lines. These would have been brought down from the GNR's Foyle Road goods yard by one of the Londonderry Port & Harbour Commissioners' locomotives.** Willie Mc Gowan collection

Above: **Derry had four railway stations in its heyday, two on each bank of the *River Foyle*, equally divided between Ireland's two main gauges. On the east side of the river was the Waterside terminus of the Northern Counties Committee line from Belfast. This was connected by a siding to the Victoria Road Station of the CDR's narrow gauge branch from Strabane. On the west side was the L&LSR's Graving Dock Station and the Great Northern one at Foyle Road. Connections, albeit tenuous ones, were provided between the four stations, by the dockside tramways of the city's port authority. The lines on either side of the river were linked by mixed gauge tracks on the bottom deck of the city's Craigavon Bridge. Wagons could only get onto these tracks by means of turntables at either end which were too small for locomotives, even dock shunters, and were hauled across the lines on the bridge by means of ropes and capstans. To work the quayside lines on the west side of the *Foyle* the LP&HC provided the locomotives. These were 5ft 3in gauge machines with buffers and drawgear which enabled them to haul wagons of either gauge. Here LP&HC 0-6-0 saddle tank No 3, built by Avonside in Bristol in 1928, is seen shunting a train headed by a 3ft gauge CDR van, in June 1937. This locomotive was subsequently preserved and is now in the care of the Railway Preservation Society of Ireland.** H C Casserley

PENNYBURN

Below: Leaving Graving Dock Station the line headed north and then swung sharply to the north-west to cross Strand Road at an angle on the level. In 1937 locomotive No 2 is bringing its train across the road and into the line's main depot at Pennyburn.
H C Casserley

Bottom left: **This unusual diamond signal, complete with lamp, controlled the crossing on one side. The complex of quayside warehouses and goods stores can be seen across the road as well as some Swilly vans and one of the company's double deck buses, in this May 1953 view.** Neil Sprinks

Bottom right: **The crossing was well-known, and often visited by photographers. Its gates were controlled from a small bothy nearby. Because of the angle at which the rails crossed the road a large bit of the latter was enclosed by the crossing gates, enough to safely park a car there anyway. Locomotive No 15 brings across a short goods bound for Letterkenny on 19th May 1950. As was the practice on the CDR, a passenger brake coach was used to accommodate the guard.**
H C Casserley

Left: **Pennyburn had an extensive range of buildings providing all th** **facilities that the railway needed. Like most other railways th** **L&LSR was loath to discard worn out items in case some further us** **could be found for them. The body of third class coach No 23, built i** **1901, was parked next to the water tower and saw service as a stor** **for many years.** H C Casserley

Centre: **Heading out of the city, the Swilly's main locomotive she** **was located opposite Pennyburn Halt.** H C Casserley

Bottom: **This halt was provided mainly for the benefit of railway sta** **with most trains calling there. Locomotive No 1 is doing just that o** **6th August 1930 with a train from Buncrana. The water tower is t** **the right. In the background looking remarkably like one of th** **early railcars of the adjoining County Donegal Railway is what mus** **have been one of the Swilly's first buses.** H C Casserley

Above: **Pennyburn shed was the principal depot of the system and it was here that all but the most major repairs and maintenance were carried out. This busy scene in front of the shed dates from May 1938. Among the locomotives in the picture are Nos 5, 8, 14 and 16. Behind No 16 on the centre road is** 0-8-0 **No 12, without its tender.** H C Casserley

Below left: **A distant view of the engine shed taken on 24th May 1953.** Neil Sprinks

Below right: **By 1953 the system was a lot less busy than it had been in 1938, Nos 10 and 15 are the locomotives recorded outside the shed in this scene taken in April of that year.** Rev R W A Jones

Above left: **The fairly nondescript setting of Pennyburn shed played host to some of the most magnificent machines ever to run on the narrow gauge in these islands. The locomotive fleet will be discussed in more detail later in the book but for the moment before leaving Pennyburn we present these fine portraits of its engines. 4-6-2 tank No 8 was built by Hudswell Clarke in 1901 and remained in service until the Swilly ended its railway operations.** John Edgington

Above right: **When this 4-6-2 tank was delivered in 1899 by Hudswell Clarke it was numbered 5. It was renumbered 15 in 1913, its original**

number going to the first of the 4-8-4 tanks which the Swilly put int service at that time. Lens of Sutton

Below: **No 2 was one of the quartet of 4-6-0 tanks built by Andrew Bar clay for use on the Burtonport line in 1902. They were officially th exclusive property of the nominally separate Letterkenny & Burton port Extension Railway and for many years carried the legend L&BEI rather than L&LSR on their tanks though these distinctions had bee forgotten by the 1950s. Here, near the end of its career, the locomo tive carried the diamond Lough Swilly logo.** John Edgington

BRIDGE END

Above: Bridge End was the first station over the border and it was here that Irish Free States customs officials checked trains. In this 1940s view the customs examination is in full swing. An officer seems to be checking the contents of one of the tank wagons at the rear of the train. Bridge End saw plenty of activity and was the focus for cross-border smuggling for many years. During the Second World War passengers from Northern Ireland travelled there for butter and other foodstuffs which were rationed at home. Getting this contraband back to Derry provided heart stopping moments for these amateur smugglers and lively entertainment for other passengers as the customs officials scoured the train. Willie McGowan collection

Centre right: No 10 with a few vans and a brake coach comprises the morning's goods train to Buncrana on 6th July 1949. The tanks were often replenished at Bridge End whilst customs clearance was going on. Willie McGowan collection

Right: Locomotive No 8 pauses at Bridge End on a goods working to Letterkenny in 1948. The story is told of bolts of cloth smuggled in from Derry being made up into suits near Bridge End and then being smuggled back for sale in the Maiden City. It's certain that there was always plenty of enterprise, both official and otherwise, in this little corner of County Donegal. Willie McGowan collection

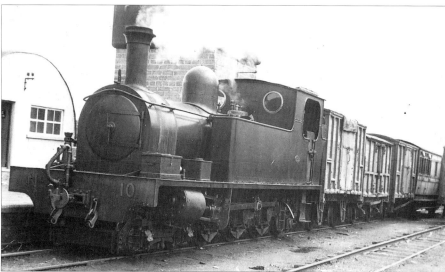

Left: **The corrugated iron structure to the left of the picture was the Customs Station. There was a siding leading to it with a crude shelter over part of this. Such inelegant constructions were once common sights along the border. The signal box at Bridge End with its distinctive single pitched roof, seen to the right of the train, was built to a standard Swilly design which was used at many locations throughout the system. Beside the signal box another old coach body has been pressed into service to provide additional storage space.** Rev RWA Jones

Below: **In April 1953 4-6-2 tank No 15 is shunting some wagons for customs examination at Bridge End.** Rev RWA Jones

Above: **No 15 simmers at the platform with the Letterkenny goods while the Customs officers do their work. From the partition of Ireland in the 1920s right up to the 1990s, commerce across the Irish border was** impeded by the delays caused by customs examinations. Of all the Irish railways the Swilly was probably the most seriously affected by the border which cut Derry off from its natural economic hinterland in the north and west of Donegal and disrupted long established patterns of trade.
Rev R W A Jones

TOOBAN JUNCTION

Right: After leaving Bridge End the line kept close to the *Skeoge River* and, after passing Burnfoot Station, made its way to Tooban Junction. When the Lough Swilly Railway was first built in 1863 it was to the Irish standard gauge of 5ft 3in and ran through to Farland Point on the Lough with a branch that headed north to Buncrana. The Farland Point line was a commercial failure and soon closed in 1866 while that to Buncrana prospered. Some 20 years later the independent narrow gauge Letterkenny Railway was built from that town to Tooban Junction where a change of trains become necessary to continue on to Derry. In 1885 the Derry to Buncrana line was re-gauged to three foot thus permitting trains from Letterkenny to run through Tooban Junction and on to Derry.

Our photo shows the point where the tracks from the platforms form the actual junction. The line to the left of the water tower is for Letterkenny and that to the right for Buncrana. Note the economical use of the one post for both starting signals. H C Casserley

Centre right: Tooban Junction was an idiosyncratic place. It had no road access, only a footpath from the lane leading to Inch Island. The station itself consisted of a simple island platform 240ft long with a signal cabin at the Derry end and, in later years, an adjoining goods store. The station site is on a long raised bank between the *Skeoge* and *Burnfoot* rivers. It was signalled and the trackwork was laid out so that trains heading in either direction could use either side of the platform. No 3 simmers at the platform in June 1950. John Edgington

Above: The station was located at the edge of the hills forming the southern end of the Inishowen Peninsula where the land reclamation work of the nineteenth century had brought many thousands of acres into use. It was always a bleak spot and the signal cabin provided a welcome respite for train crews facing the fierce winds and driving rain of the Atlantic squalls blowing up Lough Swilly. No 15 pauses with the 2.15pm goods from Letterkenny on a bright day in 1953 while awaiting the arrival of the train from Derry. H C Casserley

Top: **Trains from Letterkenny on the left and Derry meet at Tooban Junction. The rails and sleepers on the right came from the lifting of the Burtonport line.**

Centre: **The number of wagons in the trains seen in this sequence photographed in April 1953 does not bode well for the future of Swilly rail services. The costs involved in running 4-6-0 tank No 3 to Letterkenny could hardly have been met with just the revenue from the goods in the three vans behind the locomotive.**

Left: **4-6-2 tank No 8 is was in charge of the Buncrana train which seems to have more wagons than that bound for Letterkenny, a town also served by the steam hauled goods trains of the CDR at this time.**
All Rev R W A Jones

Right: **A train headed by No 10 leaves the junction bound for Buncrana, which is also our destination.** Willie McGowan collection

Below: **The line turned northwards from Tooban and passed Inch Road, the station for Inch Island, and Lamberton's Halt before entering Fahan Station. Here there was a pier at which the steamers which plied Lough Swilly called. No 8 pauses at Fahan with the goods for Buncrana in April 1953.** Rev R W A Jones

Right: **Beyond Fahan the line continued to hug the shoreline and passed two small halts before coming to Buncrana. No 10 is seen just passing the derelict Beach Halt with the 3.15pm ex-Derry on 25th March 1953. Beyond stretches the sands and golf course at Buncrana, the destination of many day trips from Derry.** Willie McGowan collection

BUNCRANA

Top left: **The 1.15pm goods from Derr**
enters Buncrana, originally the northern te
minus of the Lough Swilly Railway, on 25t
March 1953. It had a substantial layout an
was always a busy spot. In the 1920s and '30
as the L&LSR began introducing bus service
on the roads, it became a focal point for th
routes traversing the Inishowen Peninsul
Willie McGowan collection

Top right: **Buncrana Station stood an**
indeed still stands between the coast roa
and the lough shore as you enter the town.
is a fine imposing two storey building, pe
haps the finest that the company ever bui
with its intricate brickwork and imposin
windows. H C Casserley

Centre left: **There were two platforms and a**
additional running line, the gap between th
platforms recalling the standard gauge o
gins of the station. A connecting Swilly bus
parked on the platform as locomotive No
prepares to depart with the 5.07pm passe
ger working to Derry on 19th April 1948.
H C Casserley

Left: **4-6-2T No 8 is seen shunting at the Derr**
end of Buncrana Station in the late 1940
Lens of Sutton

Opposite page, top: **In their last years of se**
vice L&LSR locomotives were kept remar
ably clean, as is evidenced by the conditi
of No 10, taking water at Buncrana in 195
having brought up the goods from Derry.

Opposite bottom: **This is the view from th**
footbridge at Buncrana as No 10 runs rour
its train. The space between the platform
referred to earlier, is certainly noticeab
from this vantage point. Both John Edgingt

Top: **The platform at Buncrana was wide enough to drive a Swilly bus onto providing a very convenient road rail interchange for passengers from Carndonagh, who since the 1930s had to use the bus rather than the train. No 10 is the locomotive on the 5.10pm train to Londonderry on 15th April 1948.**
H C Casserley

Above and left: **No 8 hurries around Buncrana Station in April 1953 shunting the goods train it has just brought in.**
Both Rev R W A Jones

Right: **At the north end of the station stood the water tower alongside the turntable. It was from this point that the Carndonagh Extension was built, crossing the road and turning round the back of the town.**
Willie McGowan collection

Below: **No 10 is turned at Buncrana on the occasion when it worked a Light Railway and Tramway League special in 1953.** J H Price

Right: **The Carndonagh line was not a commercial success. Pictures of the line are few and far between. This is a heavily retouched postcard of Clonmany, one of the stations on the extension. Despite the efforts of the artist the station buildings and the signal box are definitely of L&LSR origin. The buildings at Clonmany are still in existence.**
DRRS collection

THE LETTERKENNY LINE

Top left: **Returning to Tooban Junction we shall now trace the course of the Letterkenny Railway. Leaving the junction the line ran along the top of the large embankments built earlier in the nineteenth century to reclaim the sloblands stretching south and** west of Inch Island. Some three miles of bleak open marshland brought the line to Carrowen Station, the first point where the line reached higher ground. No 15 arrives there with a short goods in April 1553.
Rev R W A Jones

Top right: **Newtoncunningham Station, viewed from the train on 24th June 1937, was an important crossing point on the run to Letterkenny. The station building was a standard Letterkenny Railway design which was used at several of the stations.** H C Casserley

Above: **There was a substantial goods store here which often required shunting by the passing trains. No 15 moves vans about the yard on 20th April 1953.** H C Casserley

NEWTONCUNNINGHAM

Above: **Newtoncunningham was a regular crossing point for trains on the line to Letterkenny and beyond. Its little signal box, by the way, has been salvaged by the CDRRS** and will be restored to its original condition. H C Casserley

Below: **The goods from Letterkenny arrives to cross that from Derry which is already at Newtoncunningham on 20th April 1953. By a remarkable coincidence two of the distinguished photographers whose work is featured extensively in this book, H C Casserley** and Rev R W A Jones, visited the Swilly in April 1953. That they both paused at Newtoncunningham at around the same time is evident from the piece of agricultural machinery left sitting near the signal box, which appears in the pictures taken by both men. Rev R W A Jones

Above: **No 15 will not be overtaxed by the load it is taking to Letterkenny that day.**

Below: **It does have a more substantial train on its return journey. That piece of machinery is still lying on the other platform as the locomotive takes water on its way back to** Derry. **One wonders how long it lay there before its rightful owner turned up to collect it. Perhaps it is still there!**
Both Rev R W A Jones

SALLYBROOK

Right: The line on from Newtoncunningham continued through rolling countryside towards the little station and dairy at Sallybrook which was a typical Letterkenny Railway structure, seen here looking back from a westward bound train on 20th April 1953.
H C Casserley

MANORCUNNINGHAM

Right: Two miles beyond Sallybrook the line came to Manorcunningham, another typical stopping place serving a small village and the surrounding rural population.
H M Casserley

Below: Manorcunningham had a goods shed and loading bay but no passing loop. A goods from Letterkenny hauled by No 15 is seen at Manorcunningham on 21st July 1952.
Desmond Coakham

LETTERKENNY STATION

Left: **No 15 shunts the goods yard at Let**
terkenny. The extremely derelict old coach
body on the platform scarcely improves the
look of the place. H C Casserley

Centre: **Letterkenny was a 24 mile and 60**
chain run from Derry. About a mile before
the station the CDR's Strabane and Let
terkenny line crossed over the L&LSR route
before running roughly parallel to it and ter
minating in its own station alongside that of
the Swilly. An interchange siding linked the

two narrow gauge systems to allow for the
transfer of goods vehicles and the running of
very occasional special trains from one sys
tem to the other. The CDR station can be
glimpsed to the right of the Swilly Station
the canopy of its island platform runs to the
right of the signal and behind the shed in the
centre right of the picture. 23rd March 195
Rev R W A Jones

Left: **Viewed from this angle which exclud**
the derelict coach bodies on the platform
the L&LSR station at Letterkenny looks qui
respectable. After the line had been close
and lifted Lough Swilly buses and lorri
continued to be based here, as can be seen
the illustration on the front cover of th
book. Rev R W A Jones

Above: **Letterkenny was a large station with substantial goods facilities. Originally a terminus it became a through station with the opening of the L&BER which commenced at the level crossing behind the train at the platform.** Rev R W A Jones

Right: **Letterkenny became a terminus again when the line to Burtonport was closed and lifted. The last rights on that epic of the Irish 3ft gauge, the erstwhile L&BER, are performed by the gang lifting the rails on the level crossing.** Willie McGowan collection

LETTERKENNY SHED

Below: **In April 1953 4-6-2 tank No 15 simmers outside the shed. Beside her is No 12, one of the pair of 4-8-0 tender locomotives acquired for use on the line to Burtonport. It looks at first glance as if the magnificent No** 12 is in steam. The steam that appears to be coming from her chimney is in fact being produced by a CDR 2-6-4 tank, whose smokebox and chimney may just be spotted to the left of the 4-8-0's smokebox. With the closure of the Burtonport line there was no longer any call for the services of No 12. The water tank which served the CDR shed can be seen behind No 12's tender. Even though they served the same county there was little co-operation between the CDR and the L&LSR. Letterkenny was the only place where through running between the two systems was possible. Rev R W A Jones

Bottom: **At the Swilly shed at Letterkenny on 23rd June 1937 No 3 has just taken on water and is about to move on to the turntable before setting back to her train.** H C Casserley

THE BURTONPORT LINE

p: The Letterkenny & Burtonport Exten-
on Railway was funded by the government
an attempt to bring some economic life to
e remote Atlantic coastal districts of west
negal and stimulate the fishing industry
providing the means for the catch to be
nsported relatively quickly to markets in
her parts of Ireland and beyond. The
BER was always a separate concern with
own locomotives and rolling stock

though worked by the Swilly. The new line
began from an end on connection with the
existing route from Derry to Letterkenny.
Our journey to Burtonport begins appropri-
ately at Letterkenny in the company of 4-8-0
No 12, a locomotive whose scale matched
that of the great, though ultimately futile,
exercise which brought the 3ft gauge to the
quayside at Burtonport. H C Casserley

Lower left: **The line ran south-west and then
westwards along several small river valleys
passing Old Town, New Mills, and Foxhall
stations before turning northwards to serve
Churchill before reaching Kilmacrenan Sta-**

tion, near to the locally renowned Holy Well
at Doon. Kilmacrenan was a typical extension line passing station with a two storey
station house, simple stone waiting room
and wooden signal box. The layout also
included a goods store and loading bank.
H C Casserley

Lower right: **The station was well fitted out.
Note the water tower, platform lamps, permanent way store and the characteristic
stone pillars of the crossing gates viewed
from a train bound for Derry on 24th June
1937.** H C Casserley

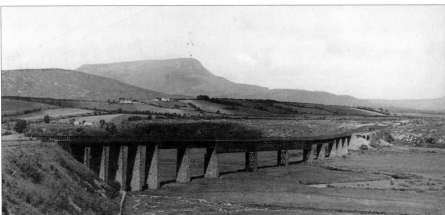

Left: **Two and a half miles further north and some 40 miles from Derry the line entered the Barnes Gap and ran alongside the post road for a mile or more before crossing it at the north end and swinging westwards. Our view shows the Gap looking to the south; the surrounding hills are granite and very forbidding. We are entering the country of high winds and bleak weather.** H C Casserley

Centre left: **After crossing the road by the viaduct at the end of Barnes Gap the railway ran along the shoulder of a hill before reaching the line's most impressive work of civil engineering, the Owencarrow Viaduct which carried the railway across the valley of the** *Owencarrow River.* **This was the scene of horrible fatal accident on 30th January 192 when a train was blown off the track in high winds. Subsequently the Swilly added extra ballast to all coaching stock and installed anemometers at Dunfanaghy Road Station nearby. These recorded a wind speed of 112mph just two years later! Some remarkable colour cine film made on this line in 1939 can be seen on Midland Publishing video,** *Irish Railways volume 3: The Irish Narrow Gauge – Colour Films 1939-1959.*
H C Casserley

Below left: **The line rejoined the coast road north of the viaduct, crossed it and dived in behind more hills through wild moorland on its way to Creeslough Station.**
H C Casserley

Photographs on the opposite page:

CREESLOUGH

Top: **Creeslough Station was the first encountered after crossing the viaduct. Built on a curve it had a passing loop, two platforms, a waiting room and signal box. The station building itself was single storied.**
H C Casserley

Centre: **The tender of No 12 is replenished with water at Creeslough on 24th June 193 She is hauling the mixed freight and passenger train, normal on the extension line (and it must be admitted, elsewhere on the L&LSR) and is about to leave for the long haul past Errigal, down to Gweedore and then out past Meenbanad to Burtonport.**
H C Casserley

Bottom left and right: **Beyond Creeslough the line again crossed the road, on the Faymore Viaduct ... before traversing wild moorland and skirting bleak hillsides on the way to Dunfanaghy Road, a station located seven miles from the village it purportedly served**
Both H C Casserley

GWEEDORE & CROLLY

Left: **Gweedore Station had the typical exten sion layout of a passing loop, two platforms signal box, water tower and goods store.** H C Casserley

Centre: **The entire Burtonport Extension wa threatened with closure in the late 1930 and some track at the Burtonport end wa lifted in 1940. This was halted because of th outbreak of war which brought about scarcity of the fuel needed for the replace ment road services. The line as far as Gwee dore, 63 miles from Derry, was reprieved Goods workings, and the occasional specia passenger service, continued until final clo**

sure in 1947. Gweedore thus became a te minus for the last few years of the Exten sion's existence. Here No 12 shunts at th station in June 1937 when closure wa already a dark cloud on the horizon. H C Casserley

Left: **From Gweedore the line headed wes wards towards the easier graded country the Rosses. Three miles on from Gweedo the line left the Bunbeg road and turne south-west to serve the little village of Crol whose station is pictured here.** Stations UK

BURTONPORT

Top and centre: **Whilst Burtonport was an important fishing port it never really produced the traffic that was hoped for. It served a small community relying on a seasonal industry and the produce from some of the poorest farmland in Ireland. In many ways it was remarkable that the line was built at all. Nevertheless Burtonport was well equipped and had a single road locomotive shed capable of taking the largest locomotives built for the line. The extension line was served by two passenger workings each day leaving Burtonport at around 8.30am and 3.20pm, taking about five hours to complete the 74 mile journey, averaging just**

under 15mph! The outward workings left ?erry at around 7.30am and 4.45pm. The ?ming varied a bit over the years. Here locomotive No 12 prepares her train of two ?aches, several vans and a brake coach in ?adiness for the 8.30am departure from ?urtonport on 24th June 1937. H C Casserley

?ght: **The end of the line at Burtonport. The ?acks ran down to the quay beyond the station which can be seen in the distance.**
C Casserley

LOUGH SWILLY LOCOMOTIVES

Below: The locomotives of the Lough Swilly Railway were a varied bunch and the company's predilection for running several numbering schemes seems to be designed to thwart the best efforts of its chroniclers. If we include the standard gauge locomotives the company owned at varying times, no less than four engines which carried the number 5. Be that as it may, the Swilly locomotive stud is a joy to review and remember. Some of Ireland's noblest narrow gauge engines ran on Swilly metals and although it may not be remembered for innovation the company can certainly lay claim to having operated some of the most powerful steam locomotives in the history of the Irish 3ft gauge. Originally, the Lough Swilly Railway was laid to standard gauge and possessed five steam engines bought between 1862 and 1879. With the amalgamation with the Letterkenny Railway in 1885 and the subsequent re-gauging, these engines were either sold or scrapped. The narrow gauge fleet began with three 0-6-2T engines supplied by Black, Hawthorn & Company in 1882/3. These were: No 1 *J.T. Mackey,* No 2 *Londonderry* and No 3 *Donegal.* They were scrapped between 1911 and 1913. The fourth locomotive was also built by Black, Hawthorn & Company. This was an 0-6-0T tank supplied in 1885. Named *Innishowen* and renumbered 17 in 1913, she lasted in service until 1940. She weighed 27 tons, carried 1¼ tons of coal and her tanks held 650 gallons of water. As No 17 this machine is seen here at Pennyburn shed on 6th August 1930.

H C Casserley

Bottom: Also in 1885 the company bought two 2-4-0Ts from the Glenariff Railway which served ironstone workings in County Antrim. They were numbered 5 and 6 but cannot have been too successful as both were scrapped in 1899. Two new locomotives were ordered from Hudswell, Clarke & Company at this time to handle the traffic on the steeply graded Carndonagh section. These 4-6-2 tanks, known as the Carn engines, were meant to be restricted to that line but despite both protests and legal action by the Board of Works they were used throughout the system. They were later renumbered 15 and 16. Here No 15 is seen at Pennyburn on 6th August 1930. H C Casserley

op left: **No16 was stored out of use under the cover of the station's oof, at the end of one of the platforms at Graving Dock, on 24th June 937. The station's wooden ticket office can be seen behind the loco-motive's cab.** H C Casserley

op right: **Perhaps the most elegant pair of Swilly locomotives were os 7 and 8, also 4-6-2Ts built by Hudswell, Clarke & Company in 901 and very similar to the 1899 pair. Near the end of her days No 7 ands inside a sunny Pennyburn shed after having her smokebox eared out. In 1903 she had the distinction of hauling the royal train hen Edward VII made a visit to Derry and for some years after car-ed the Monarch's name to mark the fact. She was scrapped in 1940.** C Casserley

entre: **No 8 exhibits classic lines outside Pennyburn shed on 6th ay 1938. With the safety valve just giving a whisper of steam she's ady for any challenge the day's work may bring.** H C Casserley

Below: **Nos 7 and 8 cost £2,060 each. Though No 7, pictured below, was cut up in 1940, No 8 lasted until closure.** H C Casserley

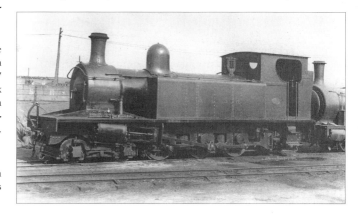

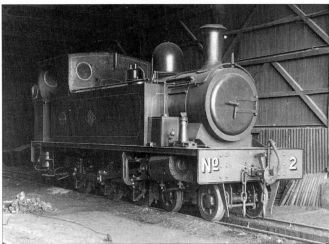

Centre left: **Chronologically, the Letterkenny & Burtonport Extension Railway now enters the fray, four locomotives being ordered from Andrew Barclay and Sons in 1902 specifically to work that line. Soon after their delivery they were working throughout the system, much to the Board of Works' annoyance, they had after all paid for them. Numbered and lettered independently of the other Lough Swilly locomotives, this separate nomenclature was officially ended in 1913, but they continued to carry the letters 'L&BER' for years afterwards. No 2, inside Pennyburn shed on 21st April 1948 had by now the L&LSR logo on her tanks.** H C Casserley

Top: **Some ten years earlier, on 24th June 1937, No 2 still carried the L&BER's lettering on her tanks.** H C Casserley

Centre right: **By contrast, No 3 seen in June 1937 at Pennyburn shed bears no letters or claim to ownership on her tanks.** H C Casserley

Bottom left: **No 4 inside the shed at Pennyburn on 15th April 1948.** H C Casserley

op: **No 3 sports the familiar LSR 'lozenge' of** ter years as she shunts vans at Tooban nction on 20th April 1953. H C Casserley

Bottom: **The last of the 4-6-0 tanks No 4, stands on one of the storage lines at Penny-burn in 1953. These 4-6-0T tanks weighed 30 tons, carried 1¼ tons of coal and 750 gallons** of water. By contrast to No 3, this locomotive was flying the flag for the erstwhile **L&BER** right up to the end. H C Casserley

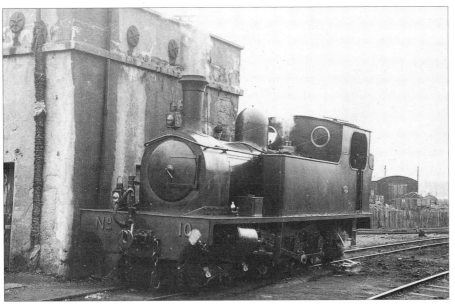

Left: 4-6-2 tanks Nos 9 and 10 were built by Kerr Stuart in 1904. They were named *Aberfoyle* and *Richmond* after the residences of two of the company's directors. They seem to have lost their nameplates during the First World War. They were ideally suited for the Derry to Letterkenny run and were known as the 'Letterkenny' engines by the loco crews. No 9 was scrapped in 1927 but No 10 survived right to the end, being finally cut up at Pennyburn in 1954. H C Casserley

Centre: 1905 saw the introduction of Ireland's only narrow gauge tender locomotives when Nos 11 and 12 entered service. These eight-coupled engines, matched to 6 wheeled tenders, were designed to handle the heaviest traffic on the system. Again the work of Hudswell Clarke, who supplied more Swilly locomotives than any other builder, they cost £2,750 each. Used mostly on the Burtonport line, No 11 survived until

1933 when she was placed on the scrap list and cannibalised to keep her sister, No 12, in operation. No 12 had not been used for some time when photographed by H C Casserley at Letterkenny in April 1953.

Left: This view of No 12 emphasises the size of this majestic locomotive. At some time in the 1940s No 12 received a home made tender cab which can be clearly seen from this angle. Whether this was solely for the benefit of crews when the loco was working tender first or was also connected with the wartime blackout regulations in Northern Ireland, an attempt to diminish the glare given off by the firebox at night, is not known.
Rev R W A Jones

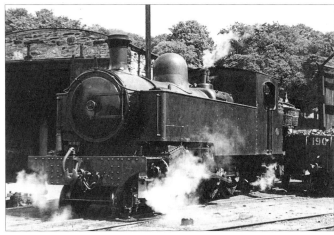

Top left: **For its penultimate pair of locomotives the company reverted to its familiar 4-6-2T format and ordered the engines from Hawthorn, Leslie & Company of Newcastle. They were delivered in 1910. Distinguished by their large side tanks which held 1,300 gallons of water, the pair were unpopular with the crews. Their high centres of gravity and all that water sloshing around in the tanks gave them a tendency to roll. Numbered 13 and 14 they both had plenty of attention from the locomotive superintendent's department. No 13 lived up to the connotations of its number and was frequently in for repair. She does not seem to have been used since 1937 and was scrapped in 1940. Her career had been an eventful one and included an incident during the Civil War in 1921 when she was derailed at Kincasslagh Road. This 1937 photograph of No 13 shows the locomotive in a siding at Pennyburn blocked in by other stock and surrounded with all sorts of junk.** H C Casserley

Top right and above: **With six years to go before its career, which was short by the standards of the longevity which distinguished many Irish narrow gauge engines, was ended, No 14 basks in the sunshine at Letterkenny shed on 24th June 1937. No 14 was also an unlucky engine. She was the locomotive hauling the train which had some of its carriages blown off the Owencarrow Viaduct in 1925. Though No 14 was undamaged in the accident, the deteriorating condition of the permanent way on the Burtonport line by the late 1930s would have exacerbated the rough riding of these locomotives and hastened their demise. No 14 lasted a bit longer than her sister, being scrapped in 1943. Interestingly, Nos 13 and 14 were two of only three locomotives which this famous firm of locomotive builders Hawthorn, Leslie & Company of Newcastle ever supplied to Irish railway companies.** H C Casserley

Below: Perhaps more than any other locomotives, the final pair to arrive on the Lough Swilly Railway in 1912 epitomised it's reputation as a big engine company. Nos 5 and 6, as they became, were built by Hudswell Clarke and were unique, the only engines with the 4-8-4 wheel arrangement anywhere in the British Isles. Here No 6 poses at Pennyburn. CDRRS collection

Bottom: They were inevitably the most powerful locomotives ever to run on the Irish narrow gauge. In terms of tractive effort they were more powerful than many engines which were running on the broad gauge lines in Ireland during the age of steam. No 5 was at Pennyburn on 19th May 1950. H C Casserley

Right: **This detailed view of the front bogie and motion of No 5 was recorded at Pennyburn in 1950.** H C Casserley

Below: **The 4-8-4 tanks weighed almost 55 tons in working order. Because of the wheel arrangement this gave the relatively low axle loading of 14 tons. No 5 pauses at Pennyburn in August 1930.** H C Casserley

Bottom left: **Nos 5 and 6 were available for service up to the end of rail services. Given the modest demands of the traffic which we have seen earlier, it is not surprising that they were not much used in their last years. When the railway closed, No 5, seen here at Pennyburn in 1953, was used to work the demolition trains which tore up the tracks it used to grace.** Midland Publishing collection

Bottom right: **What a difference a year could make to the fortunes of an engine. On 29th May 1954, No 5 was well on her way to oblivion. What a tragedy it was that none of the Swilly's magnificent quartet of eight-coupled locomotives survived a bit longer. Had they done so surely one would have been rescued for posterity.** Neil Sprinks

ROLLING STOCK
SIX-WHEEL CARRIAGES

Top: Between 1884 and 1901 the Lough Swilly acquired some 85 passenger carriages. With the opening of the L&BER a further 13 were added to the fleet. The first 22 vehicles were built by the Railway Carriage Company of Oldbury and were 6-wheelers. Their axles were of the Cleminson design which gave the wheels some side play making them more suitable for negotiating sharp curves. They were built and delivered between 1884 and 1899. Subsequent vehicles were bogie coaches built by the Lancaster Railway Carriage and Wagon Company Limited and all entered service in 1901. The L&BER carriages were bogie vehicles built by R Y Pickering of Wishaw. The coaching stock was painted a variety of colours throughout the railway's life. Originally painted dark brown above and light brown below this was replaced by black lined with red and, finally, unlined grey. The Extension Railway coaches were supplied painted cream above and crimson lake below but were made uniform with L&LSR stock when painted first black and then grey at later dates. No 2, seen here, was built as a composite offering accommodation to all three classes of passengers.
Neil Sprinks

Below: Another example of one of the early six-wheelers is No 12, also an all-third. This was an unfortunate vehicle which was maliciously derailed in 1923. It was returned to service only to be seriously damaged in the accident on the Owencarrow Viaduct in January 1925 when part of a train bound for Burtonport was blown off the rails by stron winds. Despite suffering damage includin the loss of its roof, No 12 was rebuilt in 192 and lasted up to the end of Swilly railwa operations. It was photographed at Penn burn on 21st July 1952 by Desmon Coakham.

Bottom: This side view of No 10, another vehicle from the 1884 batch, shows the three axles and general layout of the vehicle. This five compartment carriage was for the use of third class passengers only. Neil Sprinks

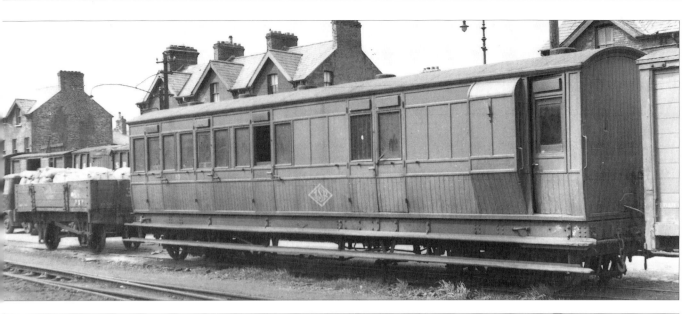

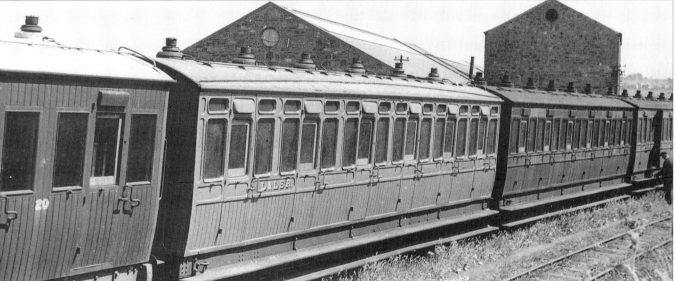

BOGIE CARRIAGES

Top: The last six-wheeler was delivered in 1899. The remaining L&LSR carriage stock was supplied in 1901 by the Lancaster Railway Carriage & Wagon Company. No 33, a brake third, was one of this batch of vehicles. It is seen here at Graving Dock in May 1951. Desmond Coakham

Above centre: 1901 bogie coaches Nos 20 and 23 were recorded at Pennyburn in 1937. No 20, nearest the camera, was rebuilt in 1925 but No 23 is in original condition. Her body was later grounded and used as a hut at Pennyburn. The Swilly's passenger coaches were lit first by oil lamps and then by acetylene generators. Eventually, most of the vehicles were fitted with electric lights running from old bus batteries. The carriages were unheated although some second-hand foot warmers were bought in the 1920s. Whether these did much good for the Swilly's long suffering passengers must be doubted. H C Casserley

Above: This view of No 31 was taken at Pennyburn in May 1951. The carriage is in original condition retaining the toplights above the windows. Many of these vehicles lost these in later rebuilds. This was a tri-composite vehicle with six compartments. When second class was abolished on the Swilly in 1929 the two second class compartments provided were re-classified as thirds. In this view the doors of the centre compartments are clearly marked '1st'. Desmond Coakham

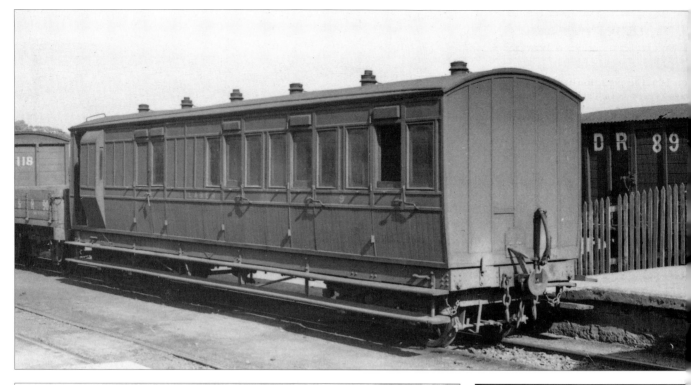

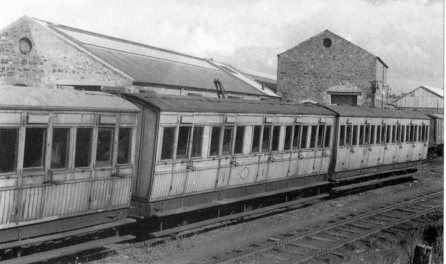

L&BER CARRIAGES

Top: **Twelve new bogie carriages wer** bought and paid for by the Board of Work for use on the Burtonport line. Numbers 1 12 were built by Pickerings of Wishaw i 1903/4, No 13 came from the same firm i 1910. They were a mixture of thirds, brak thirds and tri-composites. These carriage carried for some time the initials L&BE below the window line, as can just be seen i this picture of one of these L&BER carriage a brake third, photographed by H C Casse ley at Letterkenny on 23rd June 1937.

Centre left: **The Swilly latterly gave th** L&BER coaches the prefix 'B' before the numbers. The tri-composite on the left this rake at Derry on 19th May 1950 carrie the number B12 which is visible under th pair of windows between the two doors.
H C Casserley

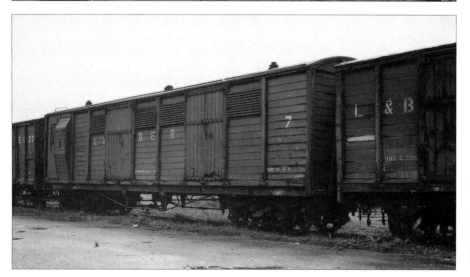

Left: **L&BER brake third carriage No 7 wa** converted in the the 1920s to a van, probab for the fish traffic which was one of the mai reasons the Burtonport line was built in th first place. The rebuild retained its brak compartment for the guard.
Willie McGowan collection

L&BER WAGONS

op right: **The extension had its own separate agon stock as well as its own carriages. Of he two L&BER wagons in this picture taken t Buncrana in July 1952, No 65 was built as a lly roofed van. No 49 was supplied with a entre canvas as seen on No 16 below but as obviously rebuilt at some time with a ll roof replacing the canvas opening.** esmond Coakham

entre right: **Three bogie vans were built for e fish traffic on the L&BER. Numbered 89 91, one of these vehicles was recorded at etterkenny on 21st July 1952.** esmond Coakham

ottom: **Out of a total of 91 wagons supplied e largest number were covered vans with a entre canvas which could be rolled back to cilitate loading and unloading. The first of ese 36 wagons was No 16. Like the L&BER rriages the wagons were built by Picker- gs.** Neil Sprinks

Above: **The L&BER had one horsebox No 6** which lasted until the end of rail services. This was a unique wagon as the Swilly never had any of these vehicles itself. H.C.Casserley

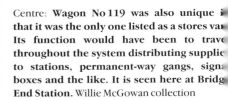

Centre: **Wagon No 119 was also unique in** that it was the only one listed as a stores van. Its function would have been to travel throughout the system distributing supplies to stations, permanent-way gangs, signal boxes and the like. It is seen here at Bridge End Station. Willie McGowan collection

Bottom left: **The stores van seen above was** renumbered 119 when it had been converted to this role from brake van No 124. This was one of six brake vans which were odd in that they were not fitted with vacuum brakes but were used to accommodate a guard or brakesman on mixed trains. The lack of brake on these vehicles rather undermined their function in this capacity. Van No 133 also started life as one of these brakeless brake vans but was later converted to a conventional covered van. It retained its original number unlike the former No 124. Desmond Coakham

L&LSR COVERED WAGONS

right: The Swilly had its own stock of wagons, theoretically kept separately from those used on the L&BER. No 58 was listed in 1925 as having been vacuum fitted and with a canvas centre to its roof. It was clearly modified to have a fully boarded roof at some stage in its career and there is no evidence of vacuum brake connections in this view of the wagon taken at Letterkenny in 1953. *Desmond Coakham*

centre right: No 55, from the same batch as No 58, retained its centre canvas until the end. Like No 58 it was supposedly vacuum fitted. Vacuum brake pipes can be clearly seen on the wagon parked behind it, but there is no trace of them on No 55. *Desmond Coakham*

below: Two Swilly and one L&BER covered vans are seen parked on a siding at Bridge End in 1953. Nearest the camera is No 123, a Swilly vacuum fitted van with the brake pipe, if not the flexible hose which should company it, in evidence. Next to it is No 58 again, which is coupled to the L&BER centre canvas wagon No 51. Several number series were duplicated in both the L&LSR and L&BER wagon lists. The Swilly No 51 was also a canvas roofed wagon. Despite the desire of the Board of Works, it must have been impossible to keep them separate even if the will to do so was there. *Rev R W A Jones*

L&LSR OPEN WAGONS

Left: **The largest part of the Swilly wagon fleet consisted of flat wagons with drop sides. No evidence survives to say which builders made these wagons, of which there was a total of 116 in 1925. No 22 has an item of farm machinery as its load at Bridge End in July 1952.** Desmond Coakham

Below: **Three flats Nos 23, 24 and 169 are loaded with oil drums at Pennyburn in July 1952.** Desmond Caokham

Bottom: **Nos 12 and 23 again are coupled up to the L&BER No 46 at Pennyburn in April 1948.** H C Casserley

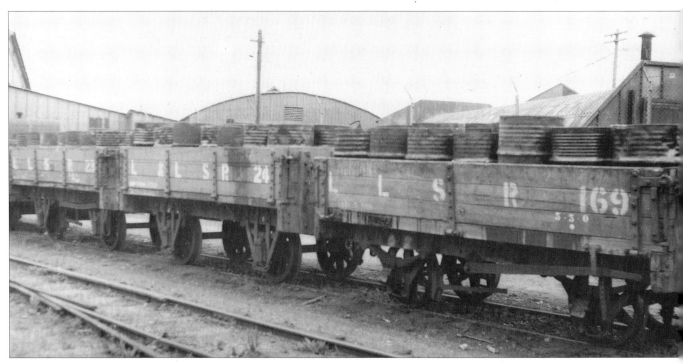

Right: When the Clogher Valley Railway closed in 1941 a number of its vehicles were purchased for use on some of the other 3ft gauge lines still in business. Perhaps the best known of these was the line's Walker railcar which became the CDR's No 10. Some CVR wagons were also acquired by the CDR to run with that line's other railcars, becoming the famous red vans, one of which can still be seen today at the Foyle Valley Railway in Derry. Some wagons also went to the Cavan & Leitrim and 12 were bought by the Lough Swilly. One of these was No 202 seen at Letterkenny in July 1952, distinguished by its corrugated iron roof. Desmond Coakham

Below: Bogie flat No 208 was the only one of its type running on the Swilly. It was built at Pennyburn in 1944 and consisted of the frame of carriage No 23 (see page 43) on

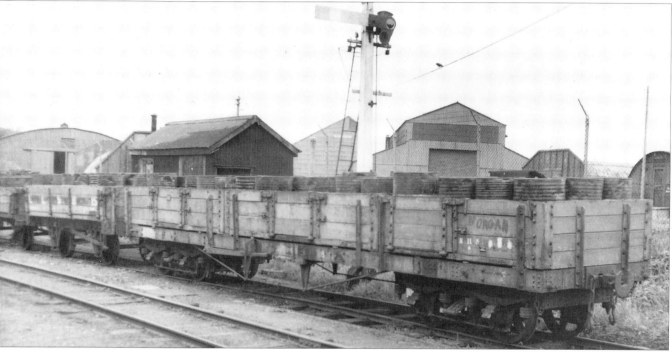

which was mounted three ex-Clogher Valley flat wagon bodies. Desmond Coakham

Right: Apart from a tenuous connection over the quayside lines at Derry, the only direct link between the L&LSR and its larger 3ft gauge neighbour in Donegal, was at Letterkenny. In this April 1953 view CDR wagons are seen at the Lough Swilly Station here. The drawgear on the wagons of the two systems were not compatible, the buffer height on L&LSR wagons was three inches lower than on Donegal vehicles. At the time of the opening of the CDR line to Letterkenny in 1909 a batch of 50 wagons built by Hurst Neilson were fitted with a modified coupling to enable them to run with Lough Swilly stock. One of these, No 264, is marshalled behind the two Swilly wagons at the head of this train. H C Casserley

Above: **The normal view of Swilly motive power, which has been repeated in this book, is that the railway was operated entirely by steam traction throughout its existence. This is not strictly speaking one hundred per cent correct as there were three small exceptions in the form of a trio of Buda-engined permanent way trollies, one of which is seen here at Bridge End in July 1952. These vehicles were acquired in 1931 at the time when the company's efforts to** develop its road transport activities were getting fully underway. Though they afforded little protection from the elements to the permanent way staff, the trollies were obviously quicker and more convenient for them than having to trudge miles along the track, through the often inclement weather of north Donegal, to get to the site of any work which needed to be done out in the wilds. Desmond Coakham

Bottom left: **Both the CDR and the Swilly carried oil in tank wagons on their tracks. Ther was a total of six of these on the Lough Swill system, five of which are seen in the siding at Derry.** Willie McGowan collection

Above: **This railway-era notice survived in bus and lorry days at Letterkenny. It shown beside the garage on the station si where road vehicle maintenance was carrie out. A Swilly Leyland Comet lorry is behin** Hugh Dougherty

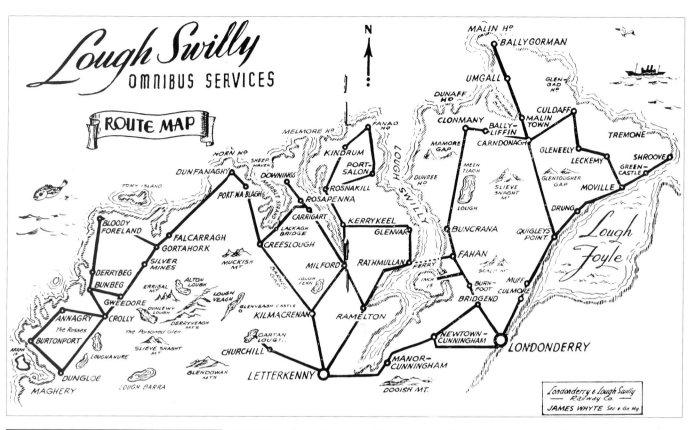

LOUGH SWILLY BUSES

The passing in 1927 of both The Northern Ireland Railways (Road Vehicles) Act and in the Free State, The Railways (Motor Road Services) Act, empowered railway companies operating on either side of the Irish border to set up road passenger and goods services to feed traffic onto their railways. The two Acts also enabled railway companies to take over competing road services in their operating areas. The L&LSR, whose rail services were in decline since partition in 1922 took full advantage of these pieces of legislation to reposition itself from being one primarily concerned with running railways to a road transport business. The first independent bus operator, Barr of Buncrana, was bought out by the Swilly in 1929, followed by a further four concerns in 1930. In 1931, when James Whyte replaced Henry Hunt as general manager of the company, more bus operators were taken over. By the end of that year the Swilly had 37 buses on its books and had also obtained its first two lorries. This brief survey will sketch the Swilly's bus operations over the years and the vehicles which it has used on those services to show how the company has contin-ued to play a significant role in the area it serve long after its railways ceased to run.

Below: One of the first buses acquired by the L&LSR was this 32-seater Vulcan. It was built in 1929 and came to the Swilly from Steele and Ferguson in Glasgow. It was in the service of the company by 1932. This was one of seven Vulcans bought to replace the motley collection of vehicles that made up the fleets of the independent operators the L&SR had taken over.

All illustrations on this page are from the Des Mc Glynn collection

Above: **The L&LSR took delivery of its first new buses in 1930. Included were a batch of seven Leylands comprising four Leyland-bodied LT1 and LT2 Lions and three Catherwood-bodied TS2 Tigers. The last two were fitted with luxurious coach bodies and were intended for touring and excursion work. One of these is seen in later years when it** had been relegated to bus duties. The vehicle is on the service from Derry to Culmore which was unusual in that it was the only Swilly bus route which did not cross the border into County Donegal.

Below: **Though the line to Carndonagh was the first part of the railway system to close,** the company's bus services continued to serve the town. This was the scene on a Fair day at Carndonagh Diamond in 1939. Lough Swilly's No 43, registration number ZA 1976, a 1934-built Leyland Cub SPK3 purchased from the Dublin United Tramway Company Limited in 1939, makes ready to leave for Moville. Hugh Dougherty collection

Top: **Between 1932 and the end of the Second World War the Swilly bought a motley collection of buses from manufacturers including Leyland, AEC, Albion and Bedford. There was even one 18-seater Morris, a firm not renowned for their bus building. Representing this period in the history of the bus fleet is No 39, a Leyland LT7 purchased new in 1938. This vehicle lasted until 1955. It is seen here at Gweedore Station on the Burtonport line. The Swilly sensibly used existing railway premises as bases for their road transport operations.** Des Mc Glynn collection

Centre left: **The former engine shed at Pennyburn had by the mid 1950s been pressed into service to hold buses and cars.** John Kennedy

Centre right: **Lough Swilly goods vehicles now used the former goods depot at Strand Road in Derry.** John Kennedy

Right: **Many of the postcards produced to extol the beauties and virtues of the Inishowen Peninsula from the 1930s onwards seemed to feature a Lough Swilly bus as part of the scenery. An unidentifiable bus leaves Moville bound for Londonderry in this view dating from that period.**
Des Mc Glynn collection

Moville from the Derry Road, Moville, Co. Donegal.

POST-WAR SINGLE DECKERS

Left: **A total of 11 buses were acquired by the Swilly in 1946, a year which saw the start of a rapid expansion of the bus fleet. One of these was No 46, a Leyland PS1, purchased from the Northern Ireland Road Transport Board.** Robert F Mack

Centre: **No 56, seen here after its withdrawal from service in 1964, was one of four AEC Regals bought in 1948. These buses had 35-seat Eastern Coachworks bodies.** Geoff Lumb

Below: **Leyland PS2/1 No 66 dated from 1949 and lasted until 1964. The bus is seen outside the former LMS/NCC Waterside Station in Londonderry. L&LSR buses were registered on both sides of the Irish border. This vehicle has a Derry City UI registration plate whereas Nos 46 and 56 above, carried County Donegal IH plates. Each country had different rates of taxation for public service vehicles and different legislation governing their operation. This covered such areas as the length of vehicles and speed limits. At one time L&LSR buses were restricted to a maximum speed of 30mph in Northern Ireland but once across the border they were permitted to travel at 35mph.** Geoff Lumb

ROYAL TIGERS

Right: **Many who remember the Swilly bus services from the 1950s through to the '70s will recall the series of Leyland Royal Tigers which formed the backbone of the fleet for many years. Eight Royal Tigers were purchased new between 1951 and 1953 and a further ten were obtained second hand from operators in England in the 1960s. The first of these buses was No 71 which arrived in 1951.** Robert F Mack

Centre: **No 78 was one of a batch of four delivered in 1953. The Royal Tigers were 44-seater buses with a centre entrance. The bodywork on these vehicles was made by Saunders Roe. They were the L&LSR 's first underfloor engined vehicles and among the first buses of this type to operate in Ireland. In 1969/70 three of the first four Royal Tigers Nos 71 to 73 were converted to front entrance which enabled them to be operated without a conductor.** Robert F Mack

Below: **The first batch of Royal Tigers were registered in Donegal, the 1953 deliveries carried Derry City plates. Like most Swilly buses of the period they had roof racks to accommodate passengers, luggage and parcels. When this was in use a tarpaulin was provided to keep the rain off items carried above. No 72 is seen on a Derry to Letterkenny service in September 1968.** Alan Roome

VARIATIONS ON A THEME

Top left: As stated earlier, a number of Royal Tigers were acquired second-hand in the 1960s from operators in England. Passengers board a service for Dunfanaghy at Letterkenny in July 1965. What was to become Lough Swilly No 97 was a Royal Tiger coach dating from 1952 when it was purchased by North Western Road Car Company in England. This had a 41-seat centre entrance body built by Leyland. The Swilly converted this to a 43-seater in 1971. In this form the vehicle lasted until 1976. Alan Roome

Top right: No 102, a 1952 built Leyland Royal Tiger with a Leyland body, bought from Ribble in 1963, kept her English registration ECK 609 when she moved across the Irish sea. She was parked outside the County Donegal Railway station at Killybegs in early August 1966 with an excursion from Burtonport to the Killybegs Sea Angling Festival. Driver Sweeny from Dungloe, right, poses with his bus while the Lough Swilly agent, from Falcarragh, out of uniform for the excursion, also gets in the frame. The 44 seater bus bears the then current grey and green livery. Hugh Dougherty

Above: No 105 was one of three Duple bodied Royal Tiger coaches built in 1952 which the Swilly obtained in 1964. They had previously been on the books of Southdown Motor Services. The first two, Nos 103 and 104 retained their 41-seater bodies but No 10 was converted by the Swilly to a 43-seater in 1971, three years before it was withdrawn Des Mc Glynn collection

TIGER CUBS

Right: **The Leyland Tiger Cubs were the Swilly's first modern front entrance buses. No 79 was one of four purchased new in 1957. The 44-seat bodies were by Weymann but they were assembled at Ryans Coach-builders in Dublin. At this time there were tax advantages in having vehicles of all types, including private cars, assembled in the Irish Republic in order to provide employment there.** Robert F Mack

Centre right: **A further four Tiger Cubs were bought new in 1960 of which No 86, seen here unloading passengers in Derry, was the last. The bodies of this batch were 43-seaters built by Dundalk Engineering who had taken over the premises of the former Great Northern Railway works in that town.** Des Mc Glynn collection

ALBION NIMBUS

Bottom left: **The last new buses bought by the L&LSR were six Albion Nimbus', delivered between 1957 and 1960. All buses acquired after these were second hand. The front entrance 31-seater bodies were built by O'Doherty in Lifford. These were the last bodies supplied to the Swilly by this famous firm which in previous decades had built railcars and trailers for the County Donegal Railway. These buses were not the most reliable and had relatively short lives. All had been withdrawn by the end of 1969. The first Nimbus, No 90, is pictured here.** Robert F Mack

Centre left: **Royal Tiger No 76 and Albion Nimbus No 91 were at Letterkenny Station in July 1965. The Nimbus is on the short route to Churchill, at one time the fourth station out of Letterkenny on the line to Burtonport.** Alan Roome

DOUBLE DECKERS

Above left: **Increasing volumes of traffic, especially on the Derry to Buncrana route, encouraged the Swilly to acquire double deckers in 1947. No 60, the first such vehicle operated by the company, was a Leyland PDIA bought new in that year. Its body was built by Alexanders and shipped in kit form to Dublin where it was assembled at CIE's Spa Road Works. No 60 remained in service until November 1968.** Robert F. Mack

Below: **Another early double decker was No 63 purchased new in 1949. This was a Leyland PD2/1 with a Leyland body and it lasted until 1972.** Robert F Mack

Above: **The Swilly added to its fleet of vintage double deckers from this early period in the 1960s when it began to acquire some second-hand vehicles from English companies. One of these was No 67 seen here about to go through the wash at Pennyburn. This bus was a Leyland PD2 with a Leyland body dating from 1952 which was purchased by the Swilly from the Birmingham and Midland Motor Omnibus Company Limited, commonly known as 'Midland Red'. This bus had the enclosed radiator which was a trademark of its former operators. It was in service with the Swilly until 1975.**
Hugh Dougherty

ove: Even older than the previous bus was 57, another Leyland PD2 which dated m 1948. It was bought by the Swilly in 63 from Ribble and lasted until 1971. n Roome

low left: Perhaps the most noteworthy of e Swilly's second-hand double deckers s their Leyland Atlantean No 87. This was

one of five demonstrators built by Leyland in 1959, the first of a long line of double deckers built on this successful rear engined chassis. The demonstrator first worked in Britain and was then passed on to the UTA and latterly CIE. It had carried three other registrations by the time it came to the Swilly in 1960. As UI 8616 it remained in service for many years with the company and

was rescued for preservation when it was finally withdrawn. No 87 is seen here in the city in September 1968 working a Derry to Buncrana service Alan Roome

Below right: In the later Swilly red and white livery the Atlantean's MCW body looks somewhat battered in this view taken near the end of its career. Des Mc Glynn collection

Opposite page top: **Lough Swilly buses continue to serve the far flung corners of north-west Donegal as the company's trains once did. In August 1973 a Royal Tiger was pictured near Burtonport on a service to Gweedore.** Hugh Dougherty

Opposite page bottom: **Since 1967 the L&LSR has provided buses for school transport under contract to the Irish government. CIE oversees this work and has since 1973 provided many vehicles on hire to the company. In the mid-1970s, near the end of its career, Leyland Royal Tiger ECK609, fleet No 102, built in 1952 and bought by the Swilly from Ribble, is seen here at Letterkenny where it has been relegated to school bus duties.** Des McGlynn collection

This page, below: **This logo was used for many years, the colours varying with the paint scheme of the vehicle to which it was applied. This bespattered example with the lower part of the circle missing, was probably used on a company lorry.** Des McGlynn collection

Photographs on this page, top to bottom:

Letterkenny has long been an important hub for the Swilly's bus operations. For many years after the CDR line serving the town closed, the buses left from the joint forecourt of the adjacent Swilly and CDR stations. The stations have since been demolished but buses still use the site. Leyland Leopard No 291 stands on the site once occupied by the platform of the CDR station. Hugh Dougherty

An impressive line up of Swilly buses parked at Letterkenny on 4th July 1993. Des McGlynn

From early on in the bus era it was common-place for some vehicles to be taken home by their drivers at the end of their duty to have them positioned near the starting point for the next day's first journey rather than have lot of wasted mileage to and from garages. This practice still continues. Leyland Leopard 254, was the bus based at Dunfanaghy in the summer of 1993. Des McGlynn

This Swilly coach was parked outside its driver's house miles from anywhere near Gweedore in the summer of 1994. The flexibility of outstation buses at locations like this cuts costs and helps to provide a better service to the company's passengers. Tom Ferris

Above: **Swilly buses continue to serve a lar part of Donegal from the west coast to t Inishowen Peninsula, the most northe part of Ireland. This bus has just arrived Dungloe in August 1970, at the conclusio a journey which has taken over four ho since leaving Derry. The seemingly ino nate time it took a steam train to get to B tonport in the past has not been grea improved by the buses which replaced** Hugh Dougherty

Centre: **The population of County Donega greatly increased with the influx of visit in summer. This puts additional pressure the buses and passenger numbers swelled during the busy summer mont Tourists are in evidence as the bus on Letterkenny/Dungloe service pauses at D fanaghy in July 1993. This service traces p of the route of the old L&BER as it pas through Barnes Gap. Observant passeng on this route can see the remains of Owencarrow Viaduct whose piers still st across the valley near Cresslough.** Des Mc Glynn

Left: **At the other end of the county, Leyla Leopard No 228 halts to pick up a passen at Clonmany in 1985 whilst working a B crana to Carndonagh service.** Hugh Dougherty

Right: There has, since the last century, been a tradition of emigration from north-west Donegal to the west of Scotland. Some of this was done on a seasonal basis linked to the demand for casual agricultural labour. Ready to bring another load of Donegal folk back to their homes, a Swilly Leyland Leopard awaits the arrival of the ferry from Stranraer at Larne Harbour in July 1980. Hugh Dougherty

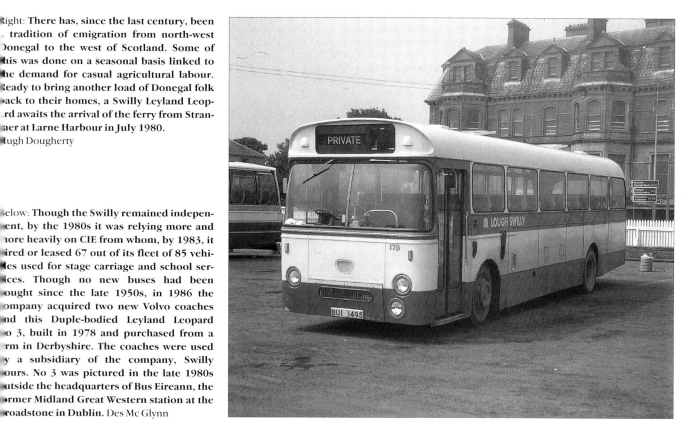

Below: Though the Swilly remained independent, by the 1980s it was relying more and more heavily on CIE from whom, by 1983, it hired or leased 67 out of its fleet of 85 vehicles used for stage carriage and school services. Though no new buses had been bought since the late 1950s, in 1986 the company acquired two new Volvo coaches and this Duple-bodied Leyland Leopard No 3, built in 1978 and purchased from a firm in Derbyshire. The coaches were used by a subsidiary of the company, Swilly Tours. No 3 was pictured in the late 1980s outside the headquarters of Bus Eireann, the former Midland Great Western station at the Broadstone in Dublin. Des McGlynn

Below: **These final views reflect the Swilly bus fleet in the 1990s. In this line up of second-hand vehicles in the company's service seen in Derry the usual mixture of British and Irish registration marks are visible. One peculiarity of LSR operations is apparent here. Swilly buses do not normally display route numbers. Where there is a route number box on a vehicle this usually displays the** fleet number of the bus as is the case with the Leyland Leopard No 312, nearest the camera. Hugh Dougherty

Bottom: **In recent years the LSR's neighbour in Northern Ireland, Ulsterbus, has proved a useful source of buses. Two ex-Ulsterbus Leyland Leopards are pictured at Derry's bus station in 1995.** Des Mc Glynn

Below: **There can be few if any other transport companies dating from the 1850s which are still in business as the 21st century approaches. The methods of providing a public transport service to the people of north-west Donegal may have changed over the years but the work of the company is still basically that which it was formed for all those years ago. The legal ownership lettering on the sides of present day buses says it all. (see below) On road fund licence disk which can be seen on the windscreens of the vehicles, the name Londonderry & Lough Swilly Railway Company, is usually spelt out in full.**

A lot of water has passed down the Foyle since the last train rumbled over the level crossing at Pennyburn in 1953 but all of those who relish the history and heritage of Ireland's railways rejoice to see this remarkable survivor head towards the millennium. Hugh Dougherty